How We Celebrate Our Fall Holidays

By Marjorie Ann Banks

Pictures — Lucy and John Hawkinson

GO

and

Supplementary

Social Studies Program

How Series

HOW HOSPITALS HELP US
HOW SCHOOLS HELP US
HOW WE CELEBRATE OUR SPRING HOLIDAYS
HOW WE GET OUR MAIL
HOW WEATHER AFFECTS US
HOW FAMILIES LIVE TOGETHER
HOW DOCTORS HELP US

HOW AIRPLANES HELP US
HOW WE CELEBRATE OUR FALL HOLIDAYS
HOW WE GET OUR CLOTHING
HOW WE TRAVEL ON WATER
HOW FOODS ARE PRESERVED
HOW WE GET OUR DAIRY FOODS

HOW WE GET OUR CLOTH
HOW WE GET OUR SHELTER
HOW WE TRAVEL ON LAND
HOW PEOPLE LIVE IN THE BIG CITY

Basic Concepts Series

HOW MAPS AND GLOBES HELP US
HOW PEOPLE LIVE IN THE MIDDLE EAST
HOW PEOPLE LIVE IN JAPAN
HOW PEOPLE LIVE IN AFRICA
HOW THE NEW WORLD WAS DISCOVERED

Photographs furnished by:

American Dental Association
American Optical Company
House of Vision, Incorporated
Weber Dental Manufacturing Company

Library of Congress
Number 61-7679

CONTENTS

LABOR DAY

It is September.

A new season will be here soon.

The trees have many colors in
their leaves.

The sky is very blue.

Many plants stop growing now.
The summer is over.
Summer work is over, too.

Many people worked hard in the summer.
They need a holiday before the new
season comes.

A holiday is a time when people
stop their work to celebrate.

First Monday
in September

Labor Day is a holiday
which working people
celebrate in September.

On this day, many people
do not go to work.

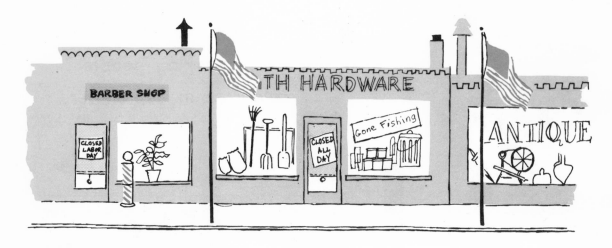

Many places of work are closed.

Other places are closed, too.

On Labor Day, people like to do things that are not work.

They rest.

They play.

Some people are in parades.

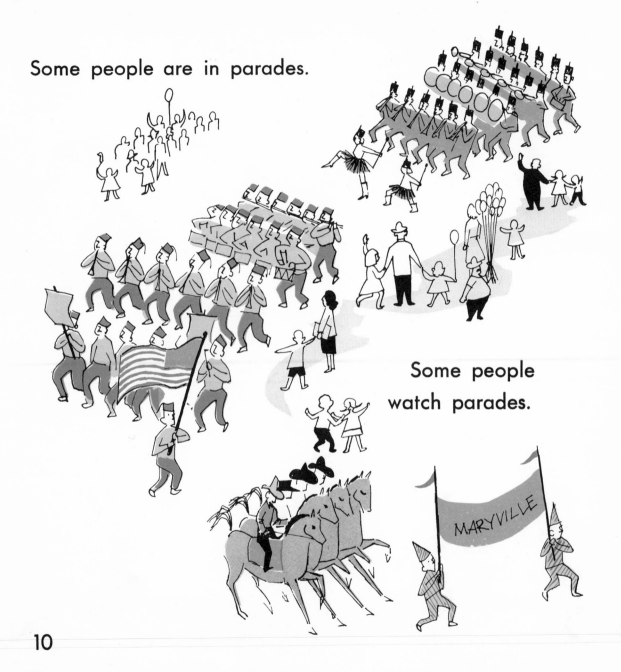

Some people
watch parades.

MARYVILLE

10

Others like to do this,

this,

or this.

11

FIRST DAY OF FALL

The new season is here!
This is a special day.
It is the first day of fall.

Leaves are falling.

Seeds are falling.

Good things to
eat are falling, too.

Animals have work to do in the fall.

Soon cold days will come.

Animals must have something to eat when the cold days come.

People have work to do, too.

FIRE PREVENTION WEEK

In the fall, we see many fires.

Fire helps people to do their work.

Fire helps people to have fun.

We must know how to use a fire.

We must know how to keep a fire
from starting.

That is why there is a special week
in October called Fire Prevention Week.

During Fire Prevention Week, there are
many special ways to learn about fire.

We learn to do this.

We learn to do this,

and this.

In school, children learn about
fires, too.

Children learn how to leave the school
when there is a fire.

They learn where to leave the school
when there is a fire.

COLUMBUS DAY

A very special day in October is Columbus Day.

Columbus Day is celebrated on October 12.

It is sometimes called Discovery Day.

On this day in 1492, Christopher Columbus found the New World.

Our country is a part of this New World.

NEW WORLD

Sailed from here

Landed here

THE ATLANTIC OCEAN

Columbus came to the New World
with three ships.

The ships were called the Nina,
the Pinta, and the Santa Maria.

Children have fun getting ready
for Columbus Day.

They have fun giving plays about
Columbus on this special day.

Some places are closed
on Columbus Day.

In some towns, there are special
Columbus Day parades.

HALLOWEEN

"Tricks or treats, tricks or treats!"
call out children on Halloween.

On Halloween, October 31, children
dress in funny ways.

They may dress like this,

or this.

Away go the children to the houses.

"Tricks or treats!" they call.

Children say they will not play tricks on people if they are given something good to eat.

Children see this
on Halloween night.

It looks funny
in the night.

Other things look funny on
Halloween night, too.

Many schools have Halloween parties.
Children help to make many things
for the party.

Some children have Halloween parties
at their houses.

Children have fun playing this

and this.

Halloween is a happy time.
Halloween is a time for fun.

VETERANS DAY

In the fall, we have a very special day for remembering people who have helped our country.

This special day is called Veterans Day.

Veterans Day used to be called Armistice Day. It was on November 11, 1918, that World War I was over.

Armistice Day became a special day to remember the ones who helped in World War I.

27

In 1954, Armistice Day became Veterans Day.

On Veterans Day, we still remember the people who helped in World War I.

And we remember all others who have helped our country at other times, too.

On this day, many of us pray for the people who have helped our country.

People watch parades on Veterans Day.
They do other special things on
Veterans Day, too.

Many people do not go
to work on Veterans Day.

Many children do not go to school.

BOOK WEEK

Children need to read good books.
They need to know where they can
get good books to read.

In November is a special week
called Book Week.

During Book Week, children can see many
kinds of good books in special places.

They like to stop and
look at the books.
They find books they
would like to read.

Children learn about good
books in other ways, too.

MARY BOYD, author of

THANKSGIVING

Long ago, in the fall of 1621, some people
in our country got ready for a special day.

It was to be a day to give thanks for
all the good things that they had.

It was to be a day of eating and singing.

The Indians came to be with these
people on this day.

This was a very special day.

This was the first Thanksgiving.

November

S M T W T F S
. . . 1 2 3 4
5 6 7 8 9 10 11
12 13 14 15 16 17 18
19 20 21 22 23 24 25
26 27 28 29 30

Thanksgiving

We, too, celebrate Thanksgiving.

Our Thanksgiving comes in November.

We get many good things ready to eat,
just as the people did long ago.

On Thanksgiving Day, many people like to be with others

to talk,

to eat,

and to have fun.

Many people pray and give thanks for

good things to eat,

a place to pray,

and good schools.

FIRST DAY OF WINTER

After Thanksgiving, the days
become colder.

The children are not cold.

They are dressed for this
new season.

The new season is winter.

Winter comes on December 21 or 22.
The first day of winter is a special day.
It is a very, very short day.
Winter days are shorter than winter nights.

CHRISTMAS

"Merry Christmas, Merry Christmas!"
call out the people.

It will soon be Christmas Day.

Christmas Day, December 25, is a
very, very special day of the year.

Children sing.

Some make good
things to eat.

Others go to find a
Christmas tree.

Schools are closed during the
Christmas holidays.

Children help to get ready for Christmas.

They help with the tree.

They help with other
things, too.

Some help so that others will have a
Merry Christmas.

Christmas is the time we celebrate the
birthday of Jesus Christ.

Many people like to go here.

They like to sing about Jesus and to
remember His birthday.

Just as some people gave
special things to the baby
Jesus, we give things to
others, too.

On Christmas Day, we go to the Christmas
tree where we find something for us.
Children look to see if Santa Claus came.
"Merry Christmas!" call the children.
Christmas is a happy time.

NEW YEAR'S DAY

A new year is coming!
People celebrate the
coming of the new year.
"Happy New Year! Happy
New Year!" they call.

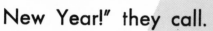

The first day of a new
year is called New Year's Day.
It is a time for fun.

New Year's Day is a time when
people think about the good things
they will do during the new year.

The old year is over.

There will be more work, holidays, and special days in the new year.

People like to think about all the things that will come in the new year.

Vocabulary

The total vocabulary of this book, excluding names of holidays and people, is 164 words. Of these, 9 are second-grade words, and 11 are above this level. The remaining 144 words are below second-grade level. In the listing below, words above second-grade level are underlined; the others are second-grade level words. The words are listed in alphabetical order, and the number indicates the page on which the word first appears.

celebrate 6	learn 16	parades 10	September 5
		part 19	ships 20
December 39		pray 29	short 39
during 16	merry 40		special 12
holiday 6	November 27	remembering 27	
			war 27
Indians 34	October 15	season 5	world 19

TEACHER'S NOTES

Holidays play an effective role in the lives of the American people. A holiday is any day on which people set aside their regular duties to do something special or to relax. Some holidays are designated as religious feast days. Days that are fixed by law for the suspension of business are deemed legal holidays.

The American people have no national holidays as such. Each state specifies the holidays it wants to observe. The United States President and Congress designate the holidays to be observed in the District of Columbia and by federal employees in all the states. The following are federal legal public holidays: New Year's Day (January 1), Inauguration Day (January 20), Washington's Birthday (February 22), Independence Day (July 4), Labor Day (the first Monday in September), Veterans Day (November 11), Thanksgiving Day (the fourth Thursday in November), and Christmas Day (December 25).

Many times special days or weeks are arranged for emphasizing definite purposes. The celebrating of special days is usually based upon the customs and traditions that have developed through the nation's cultural heritage.

The purpose of How We Celebrate Our Fall Holidays is to help children have a better understanding of the meaning and significance of our fall holidays and how they are commonly celebrated throughout the nation. However, in some areas the customs vary, due to cultural background. This being true, it is suggested that the teacher be aware of the local traditions and place proper emphasis upon them.

Notes on How We Celebrate Our Fall Holidays:

1. Labor Day is a legal holiday in honor of the working people. It is observed throughout the United States, Puerto Rico, and Canada on the first Monday in September. It was first celebrated in 1882. Later, in 1894, Congress designated the day as a legal public holiday in the District of Columbia. State legislatures proclaim it as such in their own states.

> Suggestion: Emphasize the merits and value of hard work or labor.

2. First Day of Fall, September 23, marks a change in seasons. It is a time for observation of changes in nature and in man's work and play activities. In some areas it is a time for "gathering in" or harvesting.

> Suggestion: Emphasize the changes in weather, plants, and animals. Note the changes in people's clothing and food.

3. Fire Prevention Week is observed annually on a national level. Each year the President of the United States sets aside the week that includes October 9 as Fire Prevention Week. Its history is based on the tragic Chicago Fire of October 9, 1871.

> Suggestion: Emphasize the importance of fire prevention and safety. Talk about the various equipment used to prevent and fight fires and about the importance of practicing what has been learned about fire prevention and safety.

4. Columbus Day is the anniversary of Christopher Columbus' discovery of the New World on October 12, 1492. In some states, it is called Discovery Day. It is called Fraternal Day in Alabama and Landing Day in Wisconsin. Most schools hold programs and special events on this day. Cities and organizations also sponsor special parades and banquets on this day.

> Suggestion: Bring to light some of the facts about the life of Columbus. Emphasize the courage and "never-give-up" attitude of Christopher Columbus.

5. Halloween comes on the last night in October. Its name means hallowed or holy evening, because it takes place the day before All Saints' Day. It is observed informally in the United States and is more for fun-making than any other special day during the year. Traditionally it is a time for children to have festive parties filled with make-believe characters and activities.

> Suggestion: Emphasize that this special day is an opportunity for children to release their inhibitions and engage in harmless fun and tricks. Discuss ways to have fun without harming other people's property or disturbing the peace.

6. Veterans Day (replacing Armistice Day by Act of Congress in 1954) commemorates the courage and patriotism of all men and women who have served in the United States armed forces. It is celebrated on November 11. Originally this day was proclaimed in 1919 to remind Americans of the tragedies of World War I. Many countries still celebrate November 11 as Armistice Day to commemorate the end of fighting in World War I. In the United States, Veterans Day is celebrated with special parades and

speeches. Special services are held at the Tomb of the Unknown Soldier in Arlington National Cemetery, Arlington, Virginia.

> Suggestions: Emphasize that this special day is a time to acclaim the courage, sacrifice, and heroism of those who have helped our country.

7. National Children's Book Week is a special week set aside annually about the middle of November. Its purpose is to promote the interest of young people in reading good books. Since its beginning in 1919, parents, teachers, librarians, booksellers, publishers, editors, authors, and book reviewers have joined in the annual effort to stimulate children to read. Several religious Book Weeks have developed with varying dates of observance during the year.

> Suggestion: Emphasize that books contain make-believe and factual material, that they can help meet all needs and desires, and are important treasures when selected well.

8. Thanksgiving Day originated after the first gathering of the harvest by the Pilgrims in 1621 in the New World. Governor William Bradford was responsible for setting aside that day for the feast of gathering and rejoicing. After the Revolutionary War, the feast became almost a national happening. Since the year 1863, the President of the United States has issued a proclamation to observe a day for giving thanks and praise. The day is now observed on the fourth Thursday of November. It is a genuinely traditional American holiday.

> Suggestion: Emphasize the meaning of the word "Thanksgiving" and the significance of the opportunity to express thanks, gratitude, and praise for the blessings of everyday living.

9. First Day of Winter comes about December 21. The first day of winter marks the entry of a season that is characterized by the quietness and stillness of nature. It also denotes the shortest day of the year.

> Suggestion: Emphasize how the changes in nature affect the ways of living of man and animals.

10. Christmas is a Christian festival celebrated in commemoration of the birth of Jesus Christ. It is observed on December 25 by Christians around the world. During the Christmas season people take part in religious ceremonies, decorate their homes, and exchange gifts on Christmas Eve or Christmas Day.

> Suggestion: Emphasize the spirit of Christmas. Recognize the customs that have been brought to our country, such as decorating a Christmas tree, an old German custom.

11. New Year's Day is the first day of the calendar year in our country. It is celebrated in almost every country, but the date of this celebration is not the same everywhere. Its origin dates back centuries. It was observed by the Chinese, Egyptians, Jews, Romans, Mohammedans, and early English.

> Suggestions: Emphasize that New Year's Day marks the ending of time for the past year and the beginning of time for a new year. People's resolutions to live happier and better lives during the new year are highlights of this special holiday.